Don't Be Another Girl

poems by

B.M. Owens

Finishing Line Press
Georgetown, Kentucky

Don't Be Another Girl

Copyright © 2024 by B.M. Owens
ISBN 979-8-88838-429-9 First Edition
All rights reserved under International and Pan-American Copyright Conventions. No part of this book may be reproduced in any manner whatsoever without written permission from the publisher, except in the case of brief quotations embodied in critical articles and reviews.

ACKNOWLEDGMENTS

Grateful acknowledgement to the editors and staff members of the magazines and journals where these poems from DON'T BE ANOTHER GIRL first appeared, sometimes in earlier versions or under different titles:

Jeopardy Magazine: "Clean Hands" and "A Pigeon Challenges Me in the Parking Lot"
Pittsburgh Poetry Journal: "Wishes for My Uterus"
Salamander: "The Woman Behind Me in the Target Check-Out Line"
Small Orange Journal: "Claiming the Throne"
South Florida Poetry Journal: "At 25, Britney Spears Picks Up Razor" and "My Dog Teaches Me About Self Care"

Quotes in "At 25, Britney Spears Picks Up Razor" paraphrased from *Framing Britney Spears*, "*The New York Times Presents*" documentary.

References of Harley Quinn in this book all root from the Harley Quinn DC comics, HBO Max animated series, and the film, *Birds of Prey and the Fantabulous Emancipation of One Harley Quinn*.

While pop culture references are mentioned throughout, the poems involved are wholly imaginary. Poetry, defined by Merriam-Webster, is "writing that formulates a concentrated imaginative awareness of experience in language chosen and arranged to create a specific emotional response." This chapbook is a collection of poetry, and its characters, dialogue, and events are simply vehicles driving the reader through this "emotional response." Any resemblance to actual persons, living or dead, or actual events is purely coincidental.

Publisher: Leah Huete de Maines
Editor: Christen Kincaid
Cover Art: Madari Pendas
Author Photo: B.M. Owens
Cover Design: Elizabeth Maines McCleavy

Order online: www.finishinglinepress.com
          also available on amazon.com

Author inquiries and mail orders:
Finishing Line Press
PO Box 1626
Georgetown, Kentucky 40324
USA

Contents

Don't be another girl 1

I go back to Sharon Olds 2

Wishes for my uterus 3

On rejecting inheritance 4

Self-portrait as Harley Quinn 6

When my period is late (and when it's not) 7

Daughter's internal monologue 8

My dog teaches me about self-care 10

On biting the hand that feeds you 11

Maybe this will explain my taste in furniture or why I keep walking into walls 12

An ode to the cigarette in my mother's hand 14

Clean hands 15

I'd rather walk on the highway than live with my mother (again) 17

A pigeon challenges me in the parking lot 18

"Your poems might make men uncomfortable," said a man. 19

On role play and Harley Quinn 20

At 25, Britney Spears picks up razor 22

For the men who think women don't shit 23

The whole damn farm 24

The woman behind me in the Target check-out line 26

On fetal flaws and Harley Quinn 27

Claiming the throne 29

On inosculation and sisterhood 30

On becoming trees 32

For the girls, gays, and theys.
For everyone fighting to survive in a patriarchal world
that was not meant for them.
For the family we choose along the way.

Don't be another girl

An ex told me to dress / sexier / for men // I picture the girls with breasts / he called whores / because they wore crop tops // my priest called them / ladies of the night // my mother says I won't find the right man / be a virgin / but men want sex / men want women who know how / women with undulating bodies / women with mouths / to fill // quiet women are submissive / loud women are obnoxious / screaming women are hysterical // don't be another girl / with daddy issues / my ex didn't want a woman / with issues / but men like girls with daddy issues // don't be another Owens / don't be another feminist / don't be another girl // who kisses girls / only kiss girls in front of boys / don't even befriend girls // don't be a blonde / be a blonde / not a bimbo / also be a brunette / but not basic / women must have long hair / no hair on our pussies/legs/pits/tits / use make-up / cover facial flaws / but look natural / so don't wear make-up // be tall / be short // have an appetite / but never finish a meal / or more than a serving / don't be another girl / who counts calories / don't weigh more than 135 lbs. / if she's got muscles she's a man / don't be butch / but not too femme / stay thin // have children / but don't be a mom / don't nag / but remind men / without telling them what to do // don't be another girl / who always agrees with men / have your own opinion / for men to mansplain back to you // have a role model / but not Harley Quinn // never shit / or fart / or burp / and never mention blood / period // bloody vaginas // smile through cramps / don't be fake / or passive / be passive / swallow tears / but don't be cold / wear appropriate clothes / for the weather / and exes / and men // don't be another girl

I go back to Sharon Olds

After "I Go Back to May 1937"

My therapist asks me to write
a letter to my father, but
what's the point writing the dead?
I haven't seen the point in most things
lately. But I can point to the month
I was conceived. Sharon, when did you
reach the point where you could pick up
the paper dolls of your parents and ignite
their spark? How did you let them meet
knowing they'd erupt? How do you want
to be born anyway? I'm not there.
I'm here. Building a time machine
with my words. I start at my parents'
marriage and count each month they dated—
Three. I go back to November 1991. I write
my mother and father into opposite
sides of the planet. Sew their paper feet
into the ground. Burn the hotel where
they'd meet. Smother their flame—
a defense learned from my mother.
Place her with the man she didn't marry
who wouldn't have crinkled her body—
who really was her soulmate. If
there are soulmates. Sharon,
are there soulmates? My father stays
with his first ex-wife and daughters
he'd keep choosing over my mother and I
anyway. Even in this paper place
inside my words, I know
my parents will find other ways
to be unhappy. But they won't rip each
other apart to stay/together/for/me.

Wishes for my uterus

I wish for her escape. At every gyno visit I wish the doctor would
tell me she's disappeared. I imagine the doctor pushing back my paper

gown and scrambling to find my eggs. No more pregnancy scares—
I wish her a host that wishes to see 2 solid lines on the testing stick.

But there is no transplant and my cervix is swabbed again. I don't
wish her cancer. But, maybe, just a little—caught early enough

to be an excuse. I wish her no questions—no "you'll change your mind
one day." No motherhood mantras. Carve her out. In silence. Let her rest.

With every cramp I wish her one less layer that could attract a potential
copy of my mother. I wish her hollows didn't swell—didn't nudge

when I see children. I wish she didn't dream up versions with my partner's
face. I wish thinking of broken condoms didn't turn her on—that's biology

telling me I'm almost 30. Telling me to pass on my genes. Telling me
to resist hurling the radiation apron across the doctor's room during x-rays.

I wish for her to disintegrate. To zap away any child, like me,
who wishes their mother had chosen not to give birth. I wish her

a new plot of soil—to be planted in a body that wants her.

On rejecting inheritance

I have a reoccurring dream where I'm holding a dead baby. I forgot to give
her glucose. Can babies have diabetes? Did she get it from my grandmother?
No, that was type 2. But if I had a baby, I bet she'd have diabetes. Bet

she'd wish she hadn't been born. Bet she'd have the same scowl I make—
the one my mother tries to rip off my face and can't. I can feel my mother
fighting my father through the reddened burning palm print on my cheek.

It's his cheek / his sullen mouth / his sarcasm she wants to exorcise
from my body. Maybe she thinks she can hit me hard enough to reach him.
I can understand that—that wanting to claw and tear away at the person

that pinned you down. I feel it too, surging through and into my own palms
but I stopped the spread. I took Plan B. I don't want to bring another girl
into a world where men don't hear our words, "No." No.

No, my mother was selfish to bring me into a world she didn't even want. I tell
my mother she should've married the musician from Australia, not my father.
I wouldn't have you, she hugs me, *you're going to break the Owens' curse*.

At 15, I ask my mother why some women can't have babies hoping for a spell
or ritual or practice I can use. Instead she says *some women sleep around
too much. Their bodies can't contain a baby*. She thinks I want children.

She thinks it'll stop me from having sex before marriage. It doesn't.
I fuck more men than I can count. I fuck until my ovaries are rattled. I fuck
hoping to desiccate my insides. I imagine my uterus shriveled

begging me to stop. My eggs disintegrating—maybe my unborn children
are smarter than I was—they know they'd only inherit my mother's or father's
faces. They don't want the pressure of breaking curses—real or imaginary.

My father and his father and his father's father submerged beneath drugs
and alcohol to avoid this life. My mother and her mother and her mother's
mother tried to stifle their anxieties—smother them beneath blankets.

My mother keeps hers in boxes—an ocean of cardboard spilling
into the living room, dining room, hallways, bathroom, and kitchen.
Boxes I fall over. Boxes I'm not allowed to unpack. Boxes with contents
my mother moves to every new apartment and never opens. Boxes she

asks me to carry. I opened one once—just blankets and divorce papers and receipts and printed Google searches of my father. He left us when I was 6. His father left when he was 2. At 28, I leave my mother. I have no family, only my own boxes and no child would choose to inherit this.

Self-portrait as Harley Quinn

> "I'm telling you, if you want boys to respect you, you have to show them that you're serious. Blow something up. Shoot someone. Nothing gets a guy's attention like violence."
> —Harley Quinn

Another man hurls catcalls at a woman
in a series of TikToks. She catches them
and curves their words back at them,
gentlemen, she salutes with sarcastic fingers.
She's channeling Harley Quinn
the way I wish I could. She calls them girls.
She calls their girlfriends. She calls their bluffs—
a man asks to marry her, she stops.
She steps right in front of his face,
without blinking, *Yes*. Silence.

But that's not enough—men keep talking.
Keep following. Keep touching. I want to be
Harley Quinn. Another man asks me to smile
and I laugh as a I rollerblade past him, whacking
faces off with a mallet. Another man handles my back
to walk past me. I turn to him and smile—
making sure I show off all my teeth and widen
my eyes, while igniting his beard. He drops
his hand and I toss the lighter at him. Another man
calls me dumb. I sit in his lap and say, *I have a degree
motherfucker* while cracking open his kneecaps.
Call me crazy. Call me bitch. Call me whore.
But I'll tell my story how I want. I cackle
while pulling the trigger on my "Fun Gun"—
explode bombs of glitter over men. Splatter
them in pink and purple. I'll stampede into men
with shopping carts. I'll even blow up
Ace Chemicals—any factory or men's club
or golf course just to make everyone hear me.

When my period is late (and when it's not)

For all those who supported the overturning of Roe v. Wade

I like to set the timer
and stand in front
of my microwave—
stretch just enough,
above the counter,
to feel my uterus
soak in the static
warmth of radiation.
Through the screen
I watch the bag spin—
kernels bursting
and I imagine my eggs

pop
pop
pop-
        ping

my ovaries are done.

Daughter's internal monologue

> "I'm going to pay for this poem. She has a way of making things happen. Please quit saying but she's your mother. I've never. We've never had. You don't know what it's like. I don't think you are listening."
> —Rachel McKibbens

My virtual therapist asks how I control anxiety. Isn't that why I'm here? I think of going to *Aldi* instead of eating *Taco Bell* for the third time this week. I think of diving around displays and waiting across aisles to avoid people who get too close. I think of checking out instead of ramming my cart into them like Harley Quinn—cackling as I bulldoze their bodies out of my space. How's that for controlling my anxiety? No, I can't admit this. But I can write a poem—

I tell my therapist that my mother wanted me to write her a poem. She cried when I said I'd rather buy her a pre-written card. Has anyone ever been able to control their mother? She told me to find *a professional for my anger*. I just can't contain her the way I contained my father inside boxes of lines—It's easier to idolize the dead. Of course, a poem about my father got published a week after I stopped making the effort to talk to my mother. Maybe it's my father's way of making things happen—a way to win his final custody battle. I write, "happen happen happen"

until the word loses meaning—until I can't spell it anymore. "Please complete the *Intake/Continued Therapy form*. Have you felt the need to quit drinking? Do you binge eat?" Only the Supreme *Taco Party Pack* but I need to know you longer before answering. What am I saying to my therapist? I don't remember. I tend to black out a lot but only when I speak. I can still hear my mother talking about me, *She's just like her father—She's another Owens*. Describe your relationship with your mother. She's a mother. She's my mother. Mother.

Fucker Fuck her Fuck it Fuck. Looking at my therapist, I worry I've started to hate people too—like my mother. My ex-boss liked to "joke," *#MePlease* while another boss would "compliment" my legs, but my mother couldn't understand why I quit. She's a part of the *#MeToo* movement, too, even though she doesn't know what it is and wouldn't accept it if she did. I've never tried to explain it to her. She'd say I *must have been wanting it*. That I like to expose my skin *too much*. That it's because I'm bisexual—if she knew I was bisexual. That I *drink and go to too many bars*. But even when I shrink myself into the smallest box of space in a crowded room, men find a way to place their hands on the lowest part of my back as they pass by me.

I've told men no, too. Had those men listened—if any man listened. Do men listen? Does anyone listen? "How many times have you been assaulted?" Does my therapist like listening? He gets paid to listen. People don't like what they get paid to do. It's why I chose poetry—a profession where I know I'll never make a living. People say I put too much in poems. Pick one trope. But what if they heard all my thoughts—even the ones I don't write down. It's a "24/7 therapy session" in here, The Astro Poets say, "Libras are like emotional scientists."

Should I talk about the way I forget I need to keep breathing when my dog lies just a little too still. I don't know if he's sleeping or—no, he's just sleeping. Is this session over yet? I'd rather stop thinking. Stop. Stop. Stop—My therapist looks away from the screen. How long have I been silent?

My dog teaches me about self-care

His original owners choked him—tried to contain him
to a tree with a heavy chain. Left him outside alone

with a prickly metal collar around his neck. He knew
he had to run. He still has that urge sometimes. I see

his paws bolting while he sleeps. He's still running
from that family in dreams the way I'm stumbling

away from mine. He's smarter though—he growls
and yips and tells them how their love is wrong

and tears himself out of their grasp. He extends his leg too
far and wakes himself up—a trick I have yet to learn.

He circles the bed shaking off the lingering clinch of that metal
collar cutting into his skin. His fur still hasn't grown back.

I stay awake watching him lick his paws until he's soothed
to sleep again where he dreams of foraging through

trash and chasing squirrels and sniffing every angle of every
leaf on a bush. He snores into me while my fingers comb

through his fur and I want to love smells the way
he does—I want to run towards every scent just because

it makes me happy. I want to love myself so much
I'd fracture the chain around my neck.

On biting the hand that feeds you

My mother could never afford
to get her teeth fixed—she blamed
it on needing to feed me. Genetics
and stress and smoking spaced
each tooth apart. She tends to chew
with her mouth open, smacking
together her remaining rotted molars.
I always hyper focus on my mother's
flaws. I always worry I share
my mother's flaws. I always check
my teeth for flaws. Once during
a fight, I sunk my teeth
into my mother's hand—bit
into her like a peach. Her hand
had been covering my mouth
and my instinct was to bite—
to claw myself out of her grip
and wipe her blood off my lips.

Maybe this will explain my taste in furniture or why I keep walking into walls

After Rachel McKibbens

On a cardboard box, my mother has a lamp with angels carved into the base. Its shade yellowed with mildew etching across the bottom—small enough to hide by facing it towards the wall. Whenever its bulb flickers my mother says, *That's my grandma. She's never left me.* I watch the beating light waiting to see my great-grandmother's spirit shed the electric coffin. But nothing happens. The light shifts solid again. Even at 12 I believe in Santa. Believe I have to wait 20 minutes after eating to swim. I still believe in her god—so when my mother points at the flaring lamp for proof and says *Grandma doesn't like when you act like an Owens.* I take silent tip toes back, away from the phantom hand I imagine sprouting from the lamp's top.

~

I have a doll with a spirit too—gifted after I lost my stepsister to my parents' divorce. Molly survives—5 moves / 1 dog attack / 8 years / tea parties / dress-up / forts made of cardboard boxes / missing black yarn hair / a stained blue dress / off-white socks / unbuckled shoes / a flattened red nose / odors only my mother can smell / shaped perfectly to fill the space between my arm and the flat of my bed each night.

~

During a family visit, the alive kind not the undead, my younger cousins play tag around my mother's lamp—I sit across the room watching the shade shake to the rhythm of stampeding feet. My leg bounces with the spasming light—my great-grandmother berating them. I run to stop her visage from appearing out of the lamp leaning over just too far—

I don't hear the crash but I feel the silence of my family's voices—their eyes on my fingers dangling where the lamp once rested on the box. I look down expecting smoke or mist to billow out from the glass shards—like a genie. But there is no light—holy or unholy spirit. Everyone leaves.

~

My mother tears out a garbage bag
herding me to my room,

ripping down posters
and shoving toys into the bag.
I rush to Molly,
my mother's talons reach her
first and my doll is gone—

my mother is flinging folders
from my desk, shooting books
to the other side of the room.
I don't duck when I see
the keyboard plug she threw
and I can't feel where it pierced
my forehead but I hope she broke
skin. My mother turns as blood
drips down my face.

Bandaged, I walk my *garbage*
to the chute. My mother watching
down the hall. I hug the bag
feeling for Molly's cushioned
belly—my fingers meeting
the edges and points
of the other mangled toys
mingled with pieces
of my mother's lamp inside.

She says, *You're too old
to be sleeping with dolls
anyway.* I squeeze the bag
through the pit—the sound
of crushed glass bellows down
12 floors. She hugs me, *I'm sorry.*
She doesn't want to lose my love
too. *Tell anyone who asks,
you walked into a wall.*

An ode to the cigarette in my mother's hand

Through swollen eyes
I watch each
of her trembling
fingers fumble
with the lighter.
A cigarette dangles
between her decaying
teeth. She mutters
at her bleeding knuckles
choking the lighter,
her thumb convulses
as she spins the metal
wheel while I cling
to the stained couch
praying her hair ignites.
Instead she drains
the cigarette as if
it were a glass
of her favorite wine.
She releases
a billow of words
clumsy dumbass bitch.
I swerve away but
the stench still fills
my nose. She squints
at me, the twitch in her eyes
receding. The cigarette
takes a joy ride
between her fingers
as she blesses the carpet
with ashes. Pacing
in its smog she buries
the white filter in an ashtray
with its mangled buddies.
I watch her fingers shake
with an itch, until
I see a new cigarette
in her hand and the smoke
filling the space between us.

Clean hands

Driving to a bar, I notice the bumper sticker on the car in front of me—*are you following Jesus this close?* I'd drive backwards if I could. I'd back up into the car behind me. Stop traffic. I'd back my car into a lake and still swim away backwards. I imagine driving ahead past them and saying, *don't worry I'll give Jesus all the space he needs.* Instead, I stop a car's length away behind them at a red light and look away, at my phone. My mother sends a text saying, *don't eat meat today—it's Friday.* I already had a turkey sandwich for lunch and ham for breakfast. The light changes green and I drive so slow that another car merges in front of me and grinds on Jesus' ass. My mother adds, *did you give something up for Lent?* I want to tell her that I gave up giving things up for her patriarchal god. I want to tell her that god doesn't care about us. I want to tell her that if there were an almighty god, they'd have bigger concerns than the food I eat. I want to tell her I'm going to order a bacon cheeseburger with a side of chicken wings and filet mignon for desert tonight. I want to tell her so many things, but I don't. I wait to answer. I know she'll complain later that I don't talk enough. That I don't let her in. That daughters shouldn't treat their mothers this way. That I shouldn't box myself in. That I need to let more people into my space.

At the bar a man puts his hand on my shoulder. He just wants to start a conversation, but I lean away. He doesn't step back but he puts his hands in prayer. I know he's offended. I know I'm being rude. I know I'm supposed to be grateful for his attention. I know he wants me to worship him. I know I don't want him to touch me. He says, *look my hands are clean.* If it was about clean hands, I'd spray Lysol in his face. Dunk him in detergent. Baptize him in hand sanitizer. I know that it starts at the shoulder—men want any excuse to feel for the curve of my elbow. It's an invitation to find the hollows beneath my knees. To search for the spaces between my thighs, up and under my skirt. If it was about clean hands, I'd smile and flip my hair like I'm supposed to. The way I'm expected to. The way he wants me to. Too many men have found those places before—without asking. Without permission. Without my consciousness.

If it was about clean hands, I'd go to the bathroom to wash my shoulder. I'd scrub until my skin turned raw pink, just underdone and bloody. I'd grate my nails, peeling off layers. They say it takes 28 days for skin to shed, grow an entire layer. It's been 10 years and I still feel the first hands—all of the hands—that have invaded my body. I've scrubbed down to my bones to find fingerprints etched in cartilage. How many seconds, days, weeks, years, decades does it take to erase touch from the skin?

I say nothing to the man with "clean" hands at this bar. I continue to lean away. How many men actually have clean hands? How many men ask us before grazing with their hands? How many men say nothing when they see other men reach for us? When they see us bind our bodies? I want to tell my mother I've given up letting men touch me for Lent. I've given up answering for Lent too. I'd give up this skin—give up the flesh beneath it. If I could find the right sponge, I'd scour my bones. Tonight, I don't answer the man with clean hands or my mother or anyone. I go home, picking off each fondled flake of skin from my body.

I'd rather walk on the highway than live with my mother (again)

I'd rather choose the wrong lane / a 2006 Toyota in front of me wheezing 15 mph / in a school zone / after school hours / I'd rather wait in line at the DMV / fail my driver's test / wait in line again / and fail again / I'd rather be rear-ended / left in a mangled mass of metal / I'd rather watch BMW's and Maserati's pass / unable to merge lanes / in rush hour traffic / in Miami / flooded / unable to move forward // but / it's my mother in the Toyota in front of me / crammed boxes / stacked in the backseat / blocking all windows / while balancing a tethered couch on the roof / I'd rather cram twenty toy cars / six stop signs / two brakes / into my mouth / one for each year / I lived with her / I'd rather be crammed into a toy parking garage / with only compact parking / than be in this lane / behind her / cars beeping / begging / to flow into the exit / she's beeping back / now I'm beeping / but I can't see past her boxes / into her rear-view mirror / she's inching / stopping / inching / towards the middle lane / away from the exit / no one is moving / I'd rather step out / my car still running / let another relative drive it / I'd rather walk past her / past her car / onto the exit / with no sidewalk / to protect me

A pigeon challenges me in the parking lot

She lands in front of my car—
I swear she looks at me and dares
me to run her over. I brake
and she blinks—both of us waiting
for the other to move first.
To do something—
anything.
I inch forward
and she shrugs her wings,
knowing I won't do it
or not caring—
And I get it.
I get wanting someone else
to make the choice for you—
being too tired to move
out of the way—I know
the heaviness
of a body.
I, too, imagine easing out
of flattened limbs—being the dust
that spirals from cracked bones.

        Instead she slinks
to the side, enough
to steady her body forward,
wings too weak to fly.

"Your poems might make men uncomfortable," said a man.

But that's the point—I want to set sexists on fire,
ignite the page with a lighter to watch words melt
like when I used to dangle crayons above candles
when I was a child because I could. I want to make

the "not all men" men aware of their bodies—
lose possession of their flesh the way I did
my seventh summer in a pool—floating
face up—each cell within my skin gulping

sunlight. Eyes close, while my arms and legs sift
through wave-less water. A distorted whistle
trickles into my ears. I sit up, shattering the surface.
Another whistle, louder, they shout "Hey, baby."

I look up at the building under construction. Hard
hatted men jeer and I don't know if they see I'm 7.
I cover a rounded belly and pull at my flat two-piece
bathing suit, wishing I wore a one piece or a parka.

Seven-year-olds don't know that wouldn't stop men.
I sink

      into the water waiting for the sun to set
my burning cheeks on fire like a melting red crayon.

My body dissolves
and I evaporate—

      smoke with no shape for men to grasp
I clog up through men's noses
devour the air in their throats
seep into their brains and
smolder from the inside

On role play and Harley Quinn

> *"A harlequin is nothing without her master"*
> —Harley Quinn

Google defines harlequin as *a mute character in traditional pantomime, typically masked.* But Harley Quinn never shuts up. People call her an attention seeking whore with daddy issues because she won't conform to her role—a role I've played as well. Harley breaks fourth walls. She breaks out of asylums. She breaks up with the Joker. But she's still learning—still writing her origin story. She still worries she's nothing without a man. She still doesn't know if the Joker or her parents or someone else made her a villain—Or if she became one by herself.

There's a scene in *Birds of Prey*, where Harley swallows pills and drinks and does anything and everything to help sever the link between her and the Joker. A man tells her not to cry and she remembers how to play the harlequin. Her face shifts—it's like changing masks. Her smile engulfs her face, inviting the man closer. She drinks with him to the point of unconsciousness. She wants to feel nothing. I know that numbness. The loud silence. Blackout.

The man tries to rape her in an alley and it's the only time in the movie when she barely speaks. She wants to fight but she's tired—her limbs won't move. She knows whatever she says won't stop him. I've been there too. But Harley had a witness—Black Canary finds them and throws the man through a car window while Harley slinks to the ground.

Harley sets Ace Chemicals on fire to signal the end of her role in the patriarchy and the birth of a new one. It's been years since that movie came out and I can't stop thinking about the fire—

I want to ignite / I'm fanning flames / inside my bones / purging / parts of marrow / that also whisper / I'm nothing / *without him* / flames / trickling down my arms / licking my fingers / incinerating every tissue / layer of myself / that let men order / food for me at restaurants / I'm cleansing flesh / men clutched / with permission / without permission / flames / somersaulting within / and around my blood vessels / twisting through my legs / burning off bits / that morphed / to like the same / music / movies / books / as an ex / until I forget / which bits were mine / the way Harley forgets / if she jumped into acid / or if the Joker pushed her / I forget whether a man / my mother / my father / or I / lit the match / I'm disintegrating the shadow / of me that failed / a test on purpose / to flirt with a man / flames / flinging out of my hair / embers cascading / singeing away clothes / men stitched into my skin / when they wanted to cover / my cleavage / legs / shoulders / my flames / wrapping around my naked / torso / I'm swelling / surging / billowing / ready to generate / the heat / and light / the patriarchy denied Harley / that she denied herself / my fire fuels / forges / floats up / through my spine / out of my mouth / my voice scorching / anyone who'd possess / my words / me

At 25, Britney Spears picks up razor

> *"This is a Story About a Girl Named Lucky"*
> —Brittany Spears

The buzz vibrates louder than the cameras
outside and steadies my fingers. The stylist
won't do it but I can. I'm *tired of people
touching me* anyway. I hold a strand of dyed
brown hair and release it from my head
the razor cutting through their voices,
"She must be paying the babysitters overtime."
I pull my hair ready to tear each follicle
out. I'd do it to win custody. I'd do anything.
"Girls gone wild." I drive the blade through.
"Is Britney a bad mom?" I strike again
and smile and again I'm thinking,
That's America for you. Halfway

through, I stop—the released
skin on my head breathing new air.
Cameras try to claim what's left
of my half-mullet but I won't smile
for them. The stylist says, "all the kids
are going to want to look like you"
and I think back, before my children,
to Diane Sawyer and the upset mothers
that wanted to shoot me for my lyrics,
for my clothes, for my body—
I'm not here to babysit your kids.
I guide the razor and swipe my scalp,
singeing every hair they've touched.

For the men who think women don't shit

I once held my shit in for three days
on a trip with my shitty ex-boyfriend
because he didn't believe women shit.
He didn't think women had shit
to say. Shit, he didn't even like women
saying shit
shit
        shit
shit.

My body shut down with fever
for him and I wish I had stunk up
that small hotel bathroom—
wrote on the walls with it; left
a mint sized drop on his pillow; packed
it in his suitcase between his shirts;
locked him in that room and dumped him.

The whole damn farm

I think about the first man I remember salivating at the cinnamon buns I had ordered at McDonalds. Wait, no, I hadn't gotten them yet. My mother stepped away from the cashier, covering my 8-year-old flat body. She told me that's a *bad man,* his eyes penetrating through her—the same look in the men who will grab my ass in clubs when I'm on the cusp of 18 and wearing the short skirts my mother had warned against—*You can't expect men to control themselves.* But if men want to seize us when we have no breasts, why can't we show "too much" of them now?

In elementary school boys shoved me into the sand at recess, pulling on my pigtails. I wore uniformed collared shirts, pants, and socks two inches above the ankle back then. I came home with puffy eyes and tussled hair, the women in my family told me that's just *how boys show their affection.* When I got older, I thought the bigger the bruise, the more they loved me—the more a guy used me as both sex toy and punching bag, the more I had worth.

My mother preached purity while priests crammed the Eucharist down our throats and told us to save our "ultimate gifts" for one deserving man. If we gave virginity up, what value could we offer our future husbands? I didn't want to get married at 15, or after 15, and at 15 I thought I knew everything—I unraveled my wrapping for the first boy who threw a paper ball at my head from the back of the bus and called me *beautiful.* I was too young to know I was making a statement, too young to know this wasn't what I wanted, too young to know I could tap into a power source—if I knew how to orgasm. But I didn't have an orgasm. I gave up god, while he tore open my "gift."

An ex used to dress me—the way people dress dolls growing up. As a kid, I'd press my own girl dolls together to kiss, as they wore crop tops and mini skirts, imagining a future where I could make the same choices with my own body. But my ex didn't want other men seeing the body he thought he owned. I let him pull long sweaters over my head, pushing my stiff limbs through each arm. I didn't get more tattoos because *that's not what nice girls do.* That's not how he pictured his woman walking down the aisle one day, skin rotting with ink. But I had art that wanted to surface, colors swimming through my veins—pounding, begging to breach for air.

My mother talks about men buying cows versus getting free milk—At 27 I am no cow, I'm the whole damn farm. She doesn't want to know how many cartons I've given away. I choose who plows my fields. I wonder how the first man realized they could fence us in, taking away ownership of our milk / our breasts / our bodies. Did he know we'd be too busy judging each other for the skin we each choose to air out? We become cattle waiting for men to herd us into slaughter, stripping the ink off our skin, the meat off our bones leaving us to dry, hanging from the ceiling.

The woman behind me in the Target check-out line

After the 2020 Super Bowl and the first impeachment of Trump

pulls down People Magazine asking her friend why J-Lo was wearing *that Cuban flag* during the Super Bowl. I want to tear titles off the front page—"Inappropriate & R-Rated" the way Pelosi tore Trump's State of the Union speech. Instead, I shuffle through them. The friend asks, *what was with Shakira's tongue thing?* They snicker behind white hands. I want to pelt the *Globe Magazine* at them—cram whole globes into their mouths. Could their tongues do zaghrouta then? I can't ululate either, so I bite down and place the cover of caged children singing "Born in the USA" in front of Trump's acquitted face. The woman calls J-Lo's pole dancing *soft porn*. I continue searching through the rack, "Trump's Snub to Pelosi: Intentional? Not confirmed." Where's the headline, "Trump Grabs Pussies Not Hands?" The friend asks, *Don't they know children watch the game.* I look for a shirtless Adam Levine cover from last year to throw into their carts. "Because it was the courteous thing to do considering," Pelosi quoted. She's tearing paper but I know she wants to torch the speech the way I want to set *OK! Magazine* on fire—watch the letters "Too Sexy" crumble into the next tabloid. The woman says, *I had to talk about the birds and the bees with my son after.* I hurl *Women's World Magazine's* headline "Let's Get Loud" onto their side of the conveyor belt, they gape at Shakira shackled in rope while I check out.

On fetal flaws and Harley Quinn

In movies women are mothers.
In movies, if women aren't mothers,
they wish they were mothers. In movies
women's character growth is measured
by the fertile eggs in their uteri. Try to name
one fictional woman in mainstream media
that is childless and happy and not a villain
and not killed off and not the whore—
no fatal, or *fetal*, flaw.

Black Widow is the first female lead
in the *Marvel Cinematic Universe*—after
three movies, to "humanize" the assassin,
the writers reveal Black Widow's uterus
was cut out of her. After three movies
she tells us she always wanted children.
After three movies she's a metaphor
for post hysterectomy regret.

I never liked superheroes much
anyway. I prefer the villains and anti-
heroes. An ex of mine loved comics—
I thought he'd love me as much as he loved
Batman, if I loved Batman too. But Batman
is another privileged white guy that relies on
expensive gadgets instead of going to therapy.

My ex wouldn't talk to a therapist or me
but he'd talk to a stranger about Batman.
So, I'd wander comic bookstores and find
Harley Quinn on a cover hanging Batman up-
side down with a rope tied around his ankles
and tape over his mouth. She poses with her smile
almost as wide as the entire page. Behind her,
his body swings silent with a lipstick stain
on his cheek. I'd open each of her issues:

Quinn the Harlequin
Quinn as clown
Quinn the gymnast
Quinn a babbling bimbo

Quinn the psychologist
Quinn with doctoral degree
Quinn rescues Joker
Quinn leaves Joker
Quinn as man killer
Quinn stops to take a shit
Quinn pets hyenas
Quinn as roller derby champ
Quinn befriends Poison Ivy
Quinn lover of Poison Ivy
Quinn as Bi icon
Quinn steals margaritas for her girls
Quinn a likable woman
Quinn an unlikable woman
Quinn a child-less woman
Quinn as slut
Quinn the villain
Quinn the hero
Quinn dares to be happy
Quinn dares to be alone
Quinn writes her own story

Claiming the throne

I'd say I'm a version of John Wick / killed 3 men / with a pencil / *a fucking pencil* / but as a woman / I could manage 4 / more // like I'm Harley Quinn / feeding my hyena / the hands / of men / who touch me / without permission // I'm the Wicked Witch / of the West / avenging / all my sister witches // I'm Rizzo / throwing milkshakes / in the faces of men / who don't use / condoms // Daenerys Targaryen / on my dragon / erupting / King's Landing / with fire / flying to the Iron Throne / my birthright // Regina George / men / *can't sit with us* // Maleficent / Mistress of all Evil / protecting / fairies in Moors / from men / and stealing back / wings they torn off / my shoulder blades // Queen of Hearts / for every man / who interrupts / me / *off with their heads* // I'm all 3 Sanderson Sisters / *another glorious morning* / to hang the boys / inside cages / strung from the ceiling / twirling / beneath them / cackling / because they called us / *chicks* // Bianca Stratford / I punch / his nose / at the prom / *that's for my sister* / kneeing / him in the crotch / *and that's for me* // Jennifer Check / sacrificed non-virgin / devouring / the bowels of men / for the woman I love // Ursula / Sea Witch / teaching Ariel / a voice / is more important / than any prince // I'm Lilith / think *Chilling Adventures of Sabrina* / Lilith / *I never really get the credit I deserve* / slitting / throats / of teenage boys / who force / themselves on girls / *women are taught to fear power* / I trap Satan / in a body / overthrowing / him / and his coven of men / claiming the throne / hell / for myself / for all witches / for all women / they couldn't / hang / burn / silence

On inosculation and sisterhood

I want to have roots
that crack the skulls of concrete—
to rip open sidewalks
grounded out to tame
the earth. To grow out of every
crevice in spite of anyone
who wanted to flatten me.

Inosculation occurs when one trunk or branch or root of one tree holds hands with another tree. They meld and grow together as sisters. There's a photo of an inosculated tree winding its way through Twitter—someone chopped her trunk off. Her head and upper body are suspended in the arms of her inosculated sister. No feet left to dangle or reach for the ground, the only connection to roots she has is her sister's branches. They cling to each other, refusing to die.

I should've been a tree.
Trees just know how
to continue growing—
even when chopped
or pierced, their bark
silenced, still they survive.

Google "trees that grow around things." There's a trunk sitting through a park bench, stopping anyone who'd want to sit there. A tree fingering through the scales of an abandoned piano someone left behind. Trees that should have died after a car crashed into them are growing anyway—their bark working to peel the fenders off their body, as their vines strangle the seat cushions. Trees swallow street signs whole and slice cemetery stones in half—

Trees make existing
look so easy. Their stillness
is a lie. In every second,
their cells implode
through man-made objects
while they feed and support
each other. How can I learn
to do this? How can I divide
my own cells and continue
growing in spite? How do I

inosculate with other women
or anyone stunted
by the patriarchy,
in need of extra roots—
how do we entwine
our splintered fingers?

On becoming trees

After my parent's divorce my aunt and mother started having sister days. Occasionally they'd invite me. It was just us, girls. One time we went to *Aventura mall* when I was eight and *Limited Too* stores still existed. I had convinced my mother to get me *jelly bracelets*. At the register the saleswoman told my mother her card had been declined. I didn't know my father had incinerated my mother's credit—neither did the saleswoman.

I can still picture my mother, a full force *Karen*—before we had the term, "Karen." There was a look in her eye—the kind she normally used only at home when I pushed her just too far. She screamed at the saleswoman, but I know she was really screaming at my father. I'd seen her do this to me too. Maybe she thought if she was loud enough, my father would hear her. Maybe he'd be afraid of her. Maybe this was her way of fighting back—her way of pretending she wasn't afraid of anything. But my mother couldn't see, or didn't care, how the saleswoman stepped back. How she seemed a little shorter. How she probably wanted to yell back but couldn't. How she wasn't paid enough for this.

The saleswoman called the credit card company to confirm. We waited. She handed my mother the corded phone and I started to decorate my arms with the *jelly bracelets*. I wanted to make them multiply. Bury myself beneath them. Hide.

Whatever the credit card company told my mother, she didn't like it. This memory in my mind is a soundless GIF, constantly replaying. I know my mother's voice was shrill and loud, but I can't remember what she said to the saleswoman. All I can see is my mother pelting the receiver at the saleswomen—just missing her. The phone bounces to the floor, dangling by its cord—swinging like a nearly severed branch from the body of a tree. The saleswoman clings to the counter. My aunt pulls my mother away. I try to rub the *jelly bracelets* off, but they stick to the hairs on my arms.

This moment repeats in my head, and I want to pause it. I want to alter the atoms that make up my mother. I want a different mother. I want to extend my arms, like a tree and latch on to each woman. Connect them. I want the bracelets to expand—grow beyond my fingers. I want the stillness and silence and patience of trees to inosculate all of us. Let our fibers extend into vines to a place where we can reach each other. Respect each other. Support each other. Stand still without really standing still, always listening. Our leaves shift colors together. Our branches grow together. Our roots feed together.

With Thanks

Thank you to Finishing Line Press for seeing potential in my manuscript and creating a home for this chapbook. Immense gratitude to Denise Duhamel for all her time, patience, and guidance in crafting and editing these works. I'm indebted to Julie Marie Wade for her kind feedback, ideas, and infectious good energy. Thank you to Florida International University's creative writing program and all the professors that shaped and supported my work: Maneck Daruwala, Campbell McGrath, Richard Blanco, Lynne Barrett, and Marian Demos. To Madari Pendas for steady deadlines and beautiful cover art. To Marci Calabretta Cancio-Bello for always answering the phone. To Bri Griffith for her mentorship. And to Jaden Gongaware, Jo-Anne Carrenard, Rani Ruado, Celeste Giglio, and Trey Rhone for moral support—thank you all for your friendship. To all my friends and our FIU cohort who inspire me every day. Thank you to everyone (in and out of workshops) who read several versions of my work and offered invaluable feedback. To my partner, Tyler Plum, who read more poetry than he ever has before and supported me throughout the process. This work would not exist without any of you. I love you all.

B.M. Owens is a poet and essayist who grew up in South Florida and has recently created a new home in Bellingham, Washington. Owens received her MFA in poetry from Florida International University where she also sat as Poetry and Creative Non-Fiction Editor for the Gulf Stream Magazine. Her own work has been published in *Salamander, Pittsburgh Poetry Journal, O, Miami's Waterproof Anthology, Small Orange Journal, South Florida Poetry Journal, Silk Road Review, Jeopardy Magazine,* and *Hawaii Pacific Review.* Owens was a finalist for the 2022 Academy of American Poets Prize and has been nominated for both Best New Poets and the Pushcart Prize. Her debut chapbook, "Don't Be Another Girl," was a semi-finalist in the 2022 New Women's Voices Chapbook Competition for Finishing Line Press.

www.ingramcontent.com/pod-product-compliance
Lightning Source LLC
Chambersburg PA
CBHW020220090426
42734CB00008B/1145